Pre-K ④

Animals

Contents

 Look and put the sticker.

panda

cat

monkey

dog

Let's Say

 **Put sticker on the word.**

What is it?

It's a dog .

 Ask and say.

 Color and say.

monkey

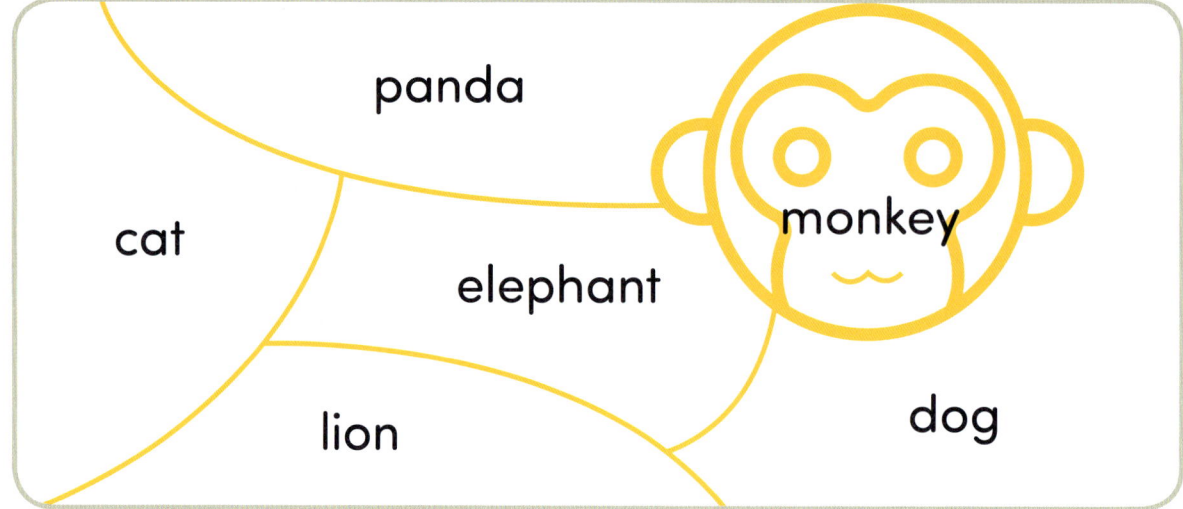

panda

cat

elephant

monkey

lion

dog

cat

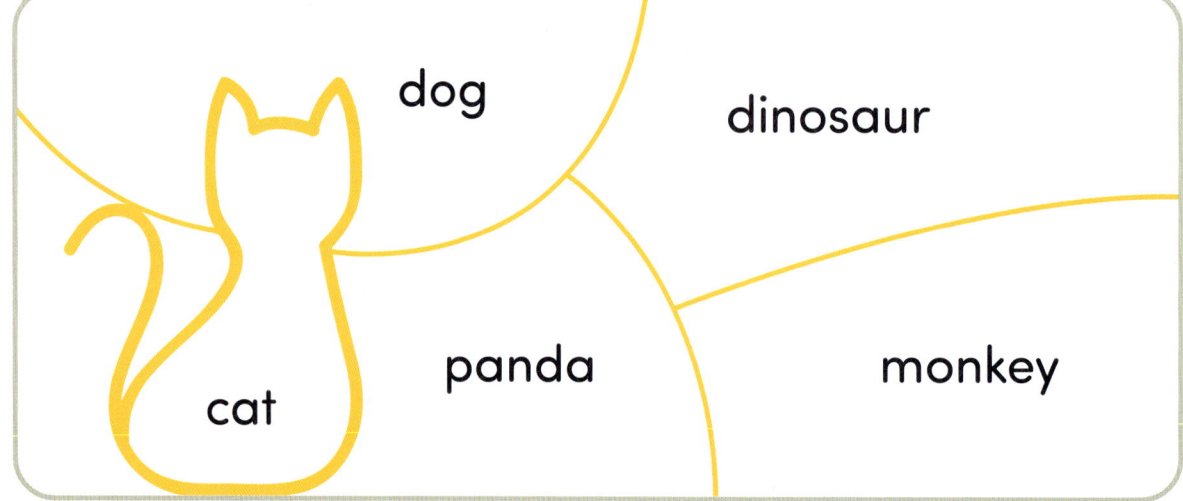

dog

dinosaur

cat

panda

monkey

 Look and put the sticker.

elephant

penguin

lion

dinosaur

 Put sticker on the word.

What is it?

It's a dinosaur .

 **Ask and say.**

 p. 2

 p. 3

dog

 p. 5

 p. 6

dinosaur

 Good work!

 Wonderful work!

 Great effort!

 For working hard!

 Good work!

 Excellent!

 Well done!

 Well done!

 Special award!

p. 8

 Sticker

Match.

cat

panda

Let's Have Fun

 Put the animal stickers.

dog

cat

lion

elephant

panda	monkey
dinosaur	penguin